Saint
Kateri
Tekakwitha

"The Lily
of the
Mohawks"

By REV. LAWRENCE G. LOVASIK, S.V.D.

Divine Word Missionary

St. Joseph Kids' Books

CATHOLIC BOOK PUBLISHING CORP.
NEW JERSEY

NIHIL OBSTAT: Daniel V. Flynn, J.C.D., *Censor Librorum*
IMPRIMATUR: Joseph T O'Keefe, *Vicar General, Archdiocese of New York*

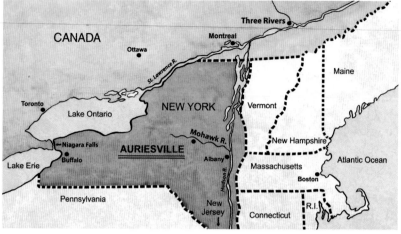

A Girl from New York State

KATERI Tekakwitha was born in 1656, a mile from the town of Auriesville, New York. This was ten years after the brave Jesuit Isaac Jogues was put to death nearby.

As a girl, she watched friendly traders and the Blackrobes, priests of New France, enter and leave the fort. The fort was known as Caughnawaga, meaning "at the rapids," because the Mohawk River runs swiftly as it passes this spot.

The Iroquois were enemies of the Huron and Algonquin tribes, as well as of the French. Kateri's mother Kahenta ("Flower of the Prairie") was an Algonquin, who had been raised and baptized near the French colony of Three Rivers in Canada.

Kateri's Mother—
A Christian from Canada

ON one of the Mohawk raids into Canada, Kateri's mother was taken through the woods and across the lakes to the shore of the Mohawk River in northeastern New York.

There Kateri came to learn about the famous "longhouses" of the Mohawks. These were made from the bark of birch trees.

Kateri's Father— A Mohawk Chief

KATERI'S mother was saved from the torture and the fire by a fierce pagan Mohawk warrior, Kenneronkwa (which means "Beloved"). She became his wife.

Like all the Mohawks, he was very tall, with fine lips, dark complexion, and straight black hair.

He was also a great hunter and warrior, skilled in using a musket and a bow and arrow, and in riding a canoe.

Birth of Kateri

THE young couple was soon blessed with a son and a daughter. The girl came later to be called Kateri Tekakwitha.

Some think the name Kateri means "Eye of the Sun."

The family lived in an Iroquois longhouse at Gandawague, a little village of the Mohawks.

Death of Kateri's Parents

WHEN the Jesuit Father LeMoyne visited the Mohawks in 1656, he found Kateri tied to her mother's cradleboard. A few years later her mother died of smallpox.

Kateri was only four years old. Her father and brother also died of smallpox, which spread like wildfire through the Mohawk nation.

Kateri herself became ill with smallpox, but she escaped death. She was then adopted by her two aunts and uncle.

When she was ten years old, war broke out between the French and the Mohawks. She fled from the village together with the other Mohawks to escape the horrors of war.

After the war, the French missionaries began to bring the Catholic Faith to the Mohawks.

Kateri's Dress and Her Works

KATERI had the well-known Indian features—high cheekbones, dull red skin, and soft dark eyes. Her well-oiled and neatly parted hair was in a long plait behind. For binding up the hair, she made ribbons and bands out of eel skins, and, for her waist, large beautiful belts.

She wore leggings and moccasins. Her dress was made of deerskins and moose skins. Beads of many colors adorned her neck. Over all she wore a red blanket.

Kateri was quiet and shy, perhaps because smallpox had made marks on her face and harmed her eyesight. When she had to go out, she shaded her eyes with a blanket.

But she was cheerful and busy. She showed special skill in making wooden things that were used in the village.

She was thin and weak from the time her mother died, and yet she was always the first one at work. She pounded the Indian corn and made the soup and gave food to the family.

Kateri Learns about Jesus

KATERI did not want to marry, though her aunts tried to force her. They began to treat her as a slave and made her do all the work that was hard.

She suffered all these insults with patience and served everybody with gentleness.

Kateri first learned about Jesus from the Jesuit missionaries. It was her duty to serve them during their visit in her uncle's cabin.

Through fear of her uncle or through shyness, she never told any missionary of her desire for Baptism for eight years.

When Kateri was nineteen years old, she injured her foot and could not leave the cabin. The missionary, Father de Lamberville, came to see her and she opened her heart to him.

*Father de Lamberville
and Kateri*

Kateri Is Baptized

AFTER Kateri was well, she began to attend the morning and evening prayers at the chapel, and to prepare for her Baptism.

She was baptized on Easter Sunday, April 5, 1676, in the chapel of St. Peter. The Indians were watching the celebration of the Great White Feast and the Baptism of the niece of a great Mohawk chief.

Kateri was now a Christian at the age of twenty, and received the name Kateri (Katherine).

Kateri's Devotion

TWICE each day she went to the chapel where the Blackrobe said morning and night prayers with his people.

On Sundays she assisted at Mass at the beautiful bark-covered chapel of St. Peter.

She also joined the Christian Indians who were chanting the prayers of the Rosary.

Kateri Bears Insults for Her Faith

KATERI'S religion was put to many tests, but she never grew weak in her faith.

Some children would pull her hair; others would point their finger at her and call her "Christian" as though they meant "dog."

Kateri's Courage in Suffering

KATERI had much to suffer from drunkards, witch doctors, enemies of Christianity, and even her uncle.

They threw stones at her and called her a witch. But she was fearless.

Voyage to a Safer Place

THE priest and some Christians of her village were Kateri's only friends, and he told her to leave the country as soon as possible. She was to go to the Praying Castle in Canada, the new Caughnawaga on the St. Lawrence River.

Having spent a year and a half in her home as a Christian, Kateri set out for the new Christian colony of Indians in Canada, which was three hundred miles away. A Christian Oneida Indian chief, known as Hot Ashes, and his wife arranged for the trip, assigning a Mohawk and a Huron brave to be her guide.

Kateri Escapes from Her Uncle

KATERI'S uncle learned that she had left and went after her to bring her back.

When Hot Ashes saw the uncle coming, he made Kateri get out of the canoe and hide in the bushes until the uncle gave up the chase. Then he put Kateri in the canoe again and paddled up the Mohawk River toward Canada.

Caughnawaga —
A Christian Indian Colony

CAUGHNAWAGA lay on the south bank of the St. Lawrence River several miles west of Montreal.

The Indian colony had about one hundred fifty families. There were sixty cabins in all with at least two families in each cabin.

Kateri Reaches Her New Home

KATERI arrived in Canada in the autumn of 1677. She gave herself to God, asking Him to do with her whatever He pleased. She was to live in the cabin of Anastasia, her mother's friend, and her brother-in-law and his wife.

Kateri brought with her a letter from Father de Lamberville to the missionaries. He had written:

"I send you Kateri Tekakwitha. Will you kindly direct her? You will soon know what a treasure we have sent you. Guard it well!

"May it profit in your hands, for the glory of God, and the salvation of a soul that is certainly very dear to Him."

The people of the village were very good Christians. Kateri enjoyed meeting the new converts. Many of them had left the country of the Iroquois. She was an example to all of them.

Kateri Makes a Friend

MARY Teresa became a close friend of Kateri. Both watched the third chapel being built, and Kateri said: "A chapel of wood is not what God wants; He wants our souls to make a temple of them."

Teresa and Kateri prayed together and did penance and shared their most secret thoughts.

Kateri was simple, humble, kind, and cheerful. She spent much time in prayer. She was obedient to the priest who was the director of her soul, but, most of all, to the Holy Spirit, Who made her soul holy.

Every morning, even in the bitterest winter, she stood before the chapel door until it opened at four and remained there until after the last Mass. There were three Holy Masses. The people prayed aloud together, especially the Rosary.

Kateri's Daily Work

KATERI kept very busy around her home. She made nets and buckets to draw water, and mats out of bark. She made clothes from skins and leather belts covered with beads.

Kateri's Devotion to Jesus in the Eucharist and on the Cross

KATERI made her first Holy Communion on Christmas in 1677 after she reached the St. Francis Xavier Mission.

Kateri was devoted to the Holy Eucharist and to Jesus Crucified. She carved the Sign of the Cross on a tree in the woods where she did her praying.

She said: "I offer my soul to Christ the Lord in the Blessed Sacrament and my body to Christ in the Lord, hanging on the Cross."

Kateri's Works of Kindness

THE people in the village liked Kateri because she was kind and cheerful in her quiet way.

Kateri walked her simple way among the people, helping with the sick, caring for the little children, and doing other works of kindness.

Kateri's Great Love for God

WHEN Kateri, a child of the forest, found God, she loved Him with her whole heart. She did everything she could to please Him, and stayed away from anything that would keep her from loving Him.

Kateri Offers Her Life to God

KATERI proved her love for Jesus by prayer and sacrifice. She would cry out: "My Jesus, I must suffer for You; I love You, but I have offended You. I am here to make up for my sins."

Kateri offered her life to God by a vow. She said to the priest: "I have dedicated myself to Jesus, Son of Mary. I have taken Him for my Spouse, and only He shall have me as a spouse."

While giving herself as a bride to Jesus, she also offered her life to the Blessed Virgin Mary, whom she loved dearly.

In memory of her consecration, she changed her scarlet blanket to blue and wore the braids of an unmarried Iroquois maiden.

She was considered a Saint by her fellow Christians because of her great love for God and all people.

Kateri Becomes Very Sick

KATERI'S health was poor. She was always in pain. She had a sickness which left her with the sweat of a slow fever and stomach pains.

Two months before Holy Week of 1680, after suffering almost a year, she felt chest pains and severe headaches. She kept herself in the same position day and night. She wanted to suffer with Jesus on the Cross.

Her greatest joy was the Holy Communion brought to her by the priest. She lived only for the love of Jesus, and now she was ready to die for Him.

On Tuesday of Holy Week, Kateri began to be very sick. She received the Holy Anointing and the Eucharist. Her friend Teresa, who was at her side, heard Kateri whisper: "I am leaving you, Teresa. I am going to die.

"Keep up your courage. Listen to the Fathers. Never give up your penances.

"I will love you in heaven. I will pray for you. I will help you."

Death of Kateri

ON April 17, 1680, Kateri died. Her last words were: "Jesus, Mary, I love You!" She was only twenty-four years old.

The Indians came to kiss her hands as she lay in death. They all said: "We have lost our Saint."

Favors Granted by Kateri

KATERI was buried at three o'clock on Holy Thursday afternoon. One of the priests said: "She loved the Holy Eucharist and the Cross, and now she can spend Holy Week in heaven."

Kateri granted many favors to those who prayed to her. The sick were cured, sinners converted, and miracles sprang up. Many Indians tried to imitate Kateri's example.

Many favors have been reported by her friends through the years. They call her the "Lily of the Mohawks."

On June 22, 1980, Pope John Paul II declared Kateri Blessed. Pope Benedict XVI declared her a Saint on October 21, 2012.

She is the first native North American Saint. Kateri of the Mohawks is the Indians' undying gift to America and the fruit of the blood of the North American Martyrs.

Prayer to Kateri

KATERI, loving child of God and Lily of the Mohawks, I thank God for the many graces He gave you. Help me to be more like you in my love for God and for people.

Give me a great love for the Holy Eucharist and the Mother of Jesus. Make me ready to make sacrifices for Jesus that I may save my soul and be happy with you in heaven.

Kateri, I love you. Always be my friend!